Developed by Nancy Hall, Inc.

Designed by Atif Toor

Ripley's images converted to 3-D by the MAGroup Bethel, CT
www.3D-Lenticular.com

ISBN 1-884270-27-1
12 11 10 9 8 7 6 5 4 3 2 1    4 5 6 7 8 / 0

Printed in Malaysia
Conforms to ASTM F963-96a

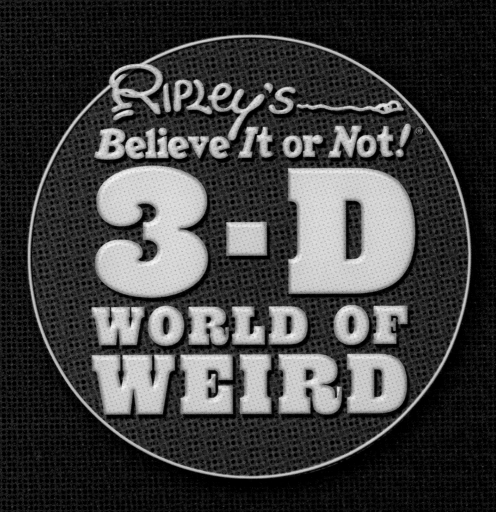

# Ripley's Believe It or Not!
# 3-D WORLD OF WEIRD

by Atif Toor

and the Editors of Ripley's Entertainment

nancy hall, inc

# YOU WON'T BELIEVE YOUR EYES!

**Welcome to the weird world of Ripley's Believe It or Not! where two-headed critters, a human unicorn, shrunken heads, and fireproof feet are just a sampling of the unbelievably bizarre items you'll come across in this book. Put your Ripley's 3-D glasses on and watch these bizarre images pop right off the pages!**

Robert Ripley began his legendary career as a collector of unbelievable facts back in 1918 when his first Believe It or Not! cartoon was published in the *New York Globe*. He initially submitted the cartoon, depicting an assortment of sports-related facts, under the title "Champs and Chumps." His editor, however, wanted a title that would reflect the extraordinary nature of the facts illustrated in the cartoons. Ripley crossed out the title and wrote "Believe It or Not!" The cartoon was an instant hit with readers and launched Ripley on a lifelong journey in pursuit of the unusual and the bizarre.

His search took him to the far corners of the globe. He visited 201 countries, traveling a distance equal to 18 trips around the world! Ripley trekked across Europe in 1920, then traveled around the world in 1923–24. In 1925, he explored South America. Ripley acquainted himself with the richly diverse cultures of every country he visited. He returned from each trip laden with unusual artifacts, costumes, and extraordinary tales to feature in his syndicated cartoons.

In 1929, cartoons depicting the curiosities Ripley discovered during his travels were compiled and published in book form. The book appeared on best-seller lists for months and was followed by several other best-selling Believe It or Not! publications. As Ripley's books were flying off the shelves, his Believe It or Not! cartoon feature was being carried in over 300 newspapers and translated into 17 different languages, reaching a readership of 80 million people worldwide.

Ripley's numerous fans also contributed regularly to his ever expanding archive of oddities. During the 1930s and '40s, Ripley received more than a million letters per year. Countless submissions included photographs and descriptions of odd farm animals, precocious pets, crazy coincidences, and reckless stunts. "All the world does my work," Ripley boasted, "and I don't have to pay 'em a cent!"

In the 1930s Ripley's Believe It or Not! items were featured on the radio, gaining instant popularity. The program went on to be a hit on television and was featured with newsreels on the big screen in movie theaters nationwide.

In 1933, Ripley assembled items from his collection and gathered many of the unusual people he had encountered to open his first Odditorium at the Chicago World's Fair. The attraction was billed as "The Greatest Oddity Show on Earth." Visitors got a firsthand look at Ripley's bizarre collection of artifacts from around the world. Some visitors fainted when witnessing the live acts by contortionists, eye-poppers, sword-swallowers, and other outrageous characters.

In the years to come, Ripley continued to shock and entertain millions through his cartoons, Odditoriums, and TV programs. Even after his death in 1949, the Believe It or Not! legacy continues with new cartoons, programs, and Odditoriums entertaining people around the world.

# ODD-INARY PEOPLE

## THE HUMAN UNICORN

A Chinese farmer known only as Weng had a 13-inch horn growing out of the back of his head. Weng disappeared from public view shortly after this photo was taken of him in Manchuria, China. Ripley offered a substantial reward to anyone who could find him again. No one ever claimed the reward.

This jovial fellow, shown here in a wax replica, was known as the Lighthouse Man of Chunking, China. He drilled a hole in his head and plugged it with a candle to light the way for visitors through the dark streets of his city. What a bright idea!

HOTHEAD

Lentini noted that every time he bought shoes, he did a good deed. Since he had to buy two pairs, he gave the extra left shoe to a one-legged friend of his.

Francesco Lentini found his third leg useful in playing soccer and launching his career in show business. Although he had three legs, they were each of different lengths. He once complained, "Yes, I have three and yet haven't a pair."

Avelino Perez had the unsightly ability to dislocate his eyeballs.  Medical experts suggest that this bizarre ability is due to shallow eye sockets. So, unless you're born with eye-popping talent, don't bother trying this at home.

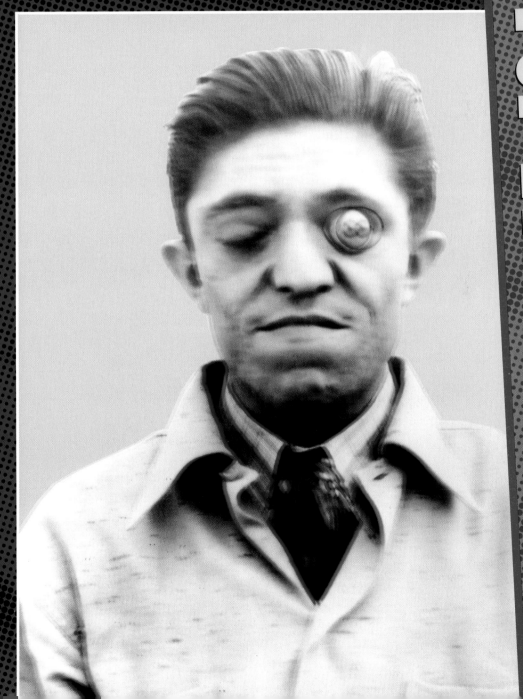

POP-EYES

# AHEAD OF HIS TIME

It took around 15 million needle jabs to cover the Great Omi from head to foot with bold black striped tattoo patterns. Omi was billed by Ripley as "the strangest looking man in the world." Omi himself insisted that "underneath it all, I'm just an ordinary man."

Eric Sprague, the Lizard Man, has undergone approximately 650 hours of tattooing in order to cover his body with scales and markings from head to toe. He's had his tongue surgically split, teeth filed to points, and bony ridges implanted in his forehead to complete the reptilian effect.

Although Jo Jo only barked and snarled in public view, he was actually fluent in four languages.

"Jo Jo the Dog-Faced Boy" suffered from a rare condition called hypertrichosis, which caused excess hair growth all over his body. Jo Jo toured Europe and the United States in various sideshows and carnivals and was a popular circus performer in the 1880s.

Martin Joe Laurello, a.k.a. "The Human Owl," amazed crowds at Ripley's Odditoriums during the 1930s with his head-turning abilities.

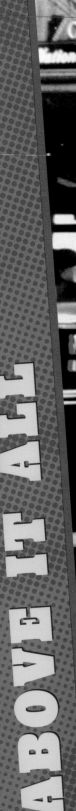

Robert Wadlow was born in 1918. He was an average-sized infant, but his size and weight increased dramatically within weeks. Wadlow reached the astounding height of six feet two inches and weighed 195 pounds by the time he was eight years old! At the age of 22, Wadlow hit eight feet eleven inches, making him the tallest person in recorded history.

Charles Stratton was a bouncing nine-pound-two-ounce baby but only grew to be three feet four inches tall. As a boy, Stratton was discovered by P. T. Barnum, who renamed him "General Tom Thumb." Tom Thumb toured Europe, charming various world leaders, including Queen Victoria, and gaining worldwide fame. He amassed a considerable fortune during his entertainment career, married 32-inch-tall Lavinia Warren, and settled in Connecticut.

SMALL WONDER

Renda Long of Glendale, Arizona, stopped cutting her nails in 1974. Needless to say, she must spend a small fortune on nail polish!

Edwin Smith was not fond of shaving, letting his beard grow for 16 years to a length of eight feet. He actually had to hire a servant to wash and comb it regularly.

The longest beard on record belonged to Norwegian Hans N. Langeth and measured 17 feet 6 inches.

# RUBBER FACE

J. T. Saylors of Villa Rica, Georgia, mastered the art of "girning," also known as swallowing your nose.

Some say the only way to be a successful girner is to wait until all your teeth fall out!

F. Velez Campos, a "dislocationist" from Puerto Rico, demonstrated his limber leg-bending ability in 1933.

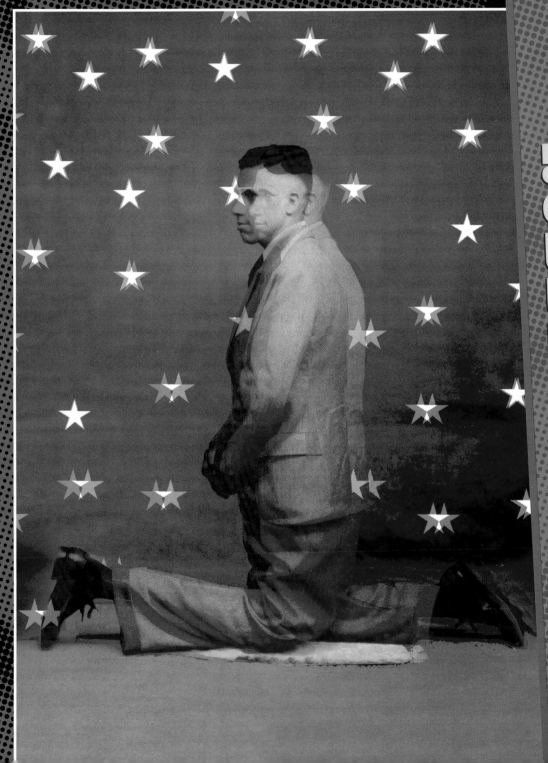

RUBBER LEGS

EXTRA! EXTRA! EXTRA!

Schoolchildren in Cross Plains, Texas, had the privilege of claiming this six-legged frog as their classroom pet.

A peculiar pooch owned by John E. Glenn had double sniffing power thanks to its extra nose.

Two-headed calves are very rare and usually don't live for more than a few hours. This one has been mounted and featured in one of Ripley's Odditoriums. Needless to say, the the double heads cause many double takes.

In the spring of 2001, a two-headed calf was delivered in Albania. Her owner initially despaired because two-headed animals legendarily brought misfortune, but her spirits were lifted when a United States Veterinary Association offered her $25,000 for it!

This atypical turtle owned by Julie Hull of Stuart, Florida, had two functional heads that could could be fed separately.

Bobby Cunningham caught a speckled trout, which held the record for being the only fish ever caught holding a record!

**Chester the Chimp is getting a ride on his custom-built water skis.**

This buggy pulled by O. J. Plomeson's prized rooster, Golden Duke, could be seen transporting Plomeson's baby daughter down Main Street in Luverne, Minnesota, back in 1910.

Ira D. Erling lost his glasses overboard while fishing. Shortly after, he caught this rock cod sporting his spectacles. Now that's a fish tale!

Weight lifting is just one of the many skills frogs can acquire under hypnosis, according to Bill Steed who founded Croaker College in Oakland, California, during the early 1970s.

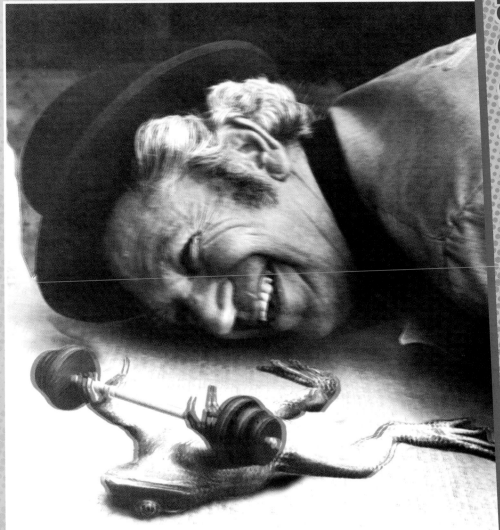

Steed's inspiration for opening Croaker College was Mark Twain's short story *The Celebrated Jumping Frog of Calaveras County.*

# TWISTED SISTER

In the late 1930s, contortionist Alma Ynclan of Tampa, Florida, was featured in several Ripley cartoons for her astounding ability to fold herself into a pretzel.

Doing a headstand is impressive but sitting on your own head takes true talent. Lorraine Chevalier, of the famous Chevalier family of acrobats, demonstrates her unbelievable ability in this photo taken in 1937.

In 1948, Jacqueline Terry wasn't content with just sitting on her own head. She managed to do it while supporting her entire weight with her jaws.

Dotzauer was known as "the Human Seal" for his extraordinary balancing abilities.

In 1953, Robert Dotzauer managed to balance three iron lawn mowers weighing a total of 150 pounds on his chin. Some people will do anything to avoid cutting the grass!

Two tables and six chairs in one bite! Five-foot-tall Jackie Del Rio could also lift a seated person in a chair with his mighty molars.

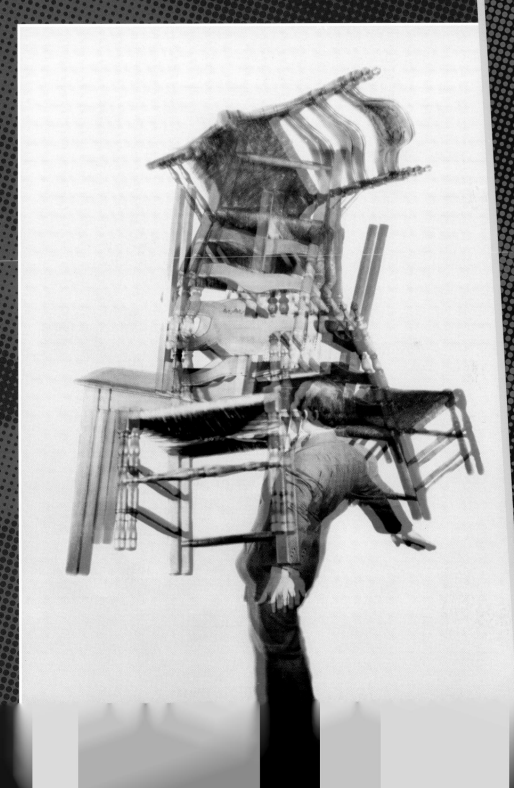

HAVE A SEAT!

Lena Deeter of Conway, Arkansas, could write with both hands at the same time. Not impressed? She could also simultaneously write backward, forward, upside down, and upside down and backward.

Clarence Thorpe of Augusta, Kansas, could draw two different pictures at the same time using his hand to draw one and his foot to draw the other. Thorpe could also draw cartoons while blindfolded!

A one-man band, Simon Pagani could play the accordion, cello, and whistle all at the same time. The blind musician could be found wowing audiences around his hometown of LaSalle, Illinois.

James Paul, a.k.a. "the Greek Titan," claimed he suffered from weak teeth until he was given a special remedy in Cypress, Greece. His weak teeth not only recovered, they managed to lift six people weighing a total of 735 pounds.

Tough-as-nails sideshow performer Francois Russell could pull nails out of wood blocks with his teeth.

"Little Giant" Eddie Polo weighed just 135 pounds but mustered the Herculean strength to pull a car by his hair for 100 yards in 1937.

On the same day as his hair-pulling feat, Eddie Polo broke chains with his chest, bent steel bars, and beat eight men pulling together against him in a tug-of-war.

# ONE SPRY GUY

Perry L. Biddle demonstrates that you're never too old to reinvent yourself. He hoisted himself up to become a human flag on his 90th birthday in 1936.

Renee DeLue loved to accessorize her outfits with a little help from her acrobatic partner, Ruby Dale, who wrapped herself into a human belt for awestruck audiences in 1946.

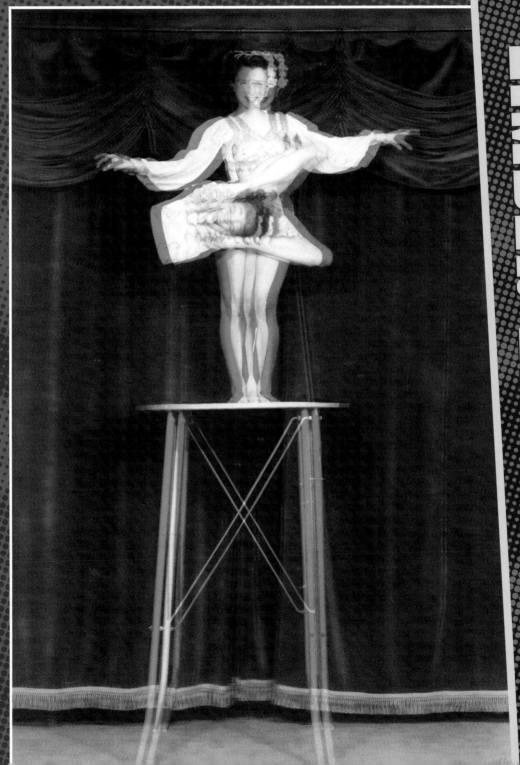

# HEADSTRONG

Evans's heavyweight head-balancing has caused him to shrink. He's lost two inches off his six foot two inch height!

Aside from balancing a small car on his head, John Evans's head-balancing accomplishments include 101 bricks, 400 cans of soda, and 11 beer kegs. "My neighbors thought I was weird at first," admits John, "but I'm renowned for it now all over the world."

Entertainer Alexandre Patty demonstrates his unconventional stair-climbing method in 1928.

35

# TONGUE-LASHING

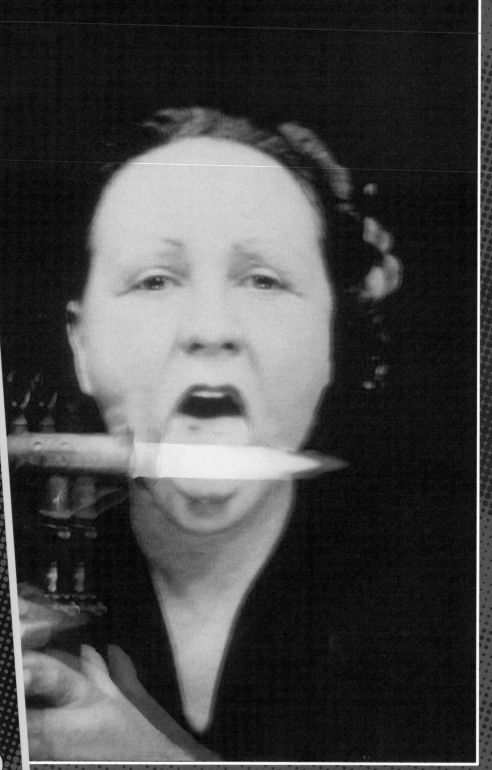

Leona Young called herself "the Devil's Daughter" because of her heat-defying ability to apply a blowtorch to her tongue. She stunned audiences with her performances, using torches, molten lead, and explosives against her bare skin.

On August 16, 1938, a fiery pit was prepared outside Radio City Music Hall in New York. After burning for several hours, the temperature reached a scorching 1220°F. The crowd gasped as Kuda Bux of Kashmir, India, walked through the pit barefoot, sinking up to his ankles in the white-hot coals. Doctors standing by examined Bux's feet and found them miraculously unharmed.

Kuda Bux was also known as "The Man with the X-ray Eyes" because he once rode a bicycle around Manhattan while blindfolded!

FIREPROOF FEET

**HEAD SET**

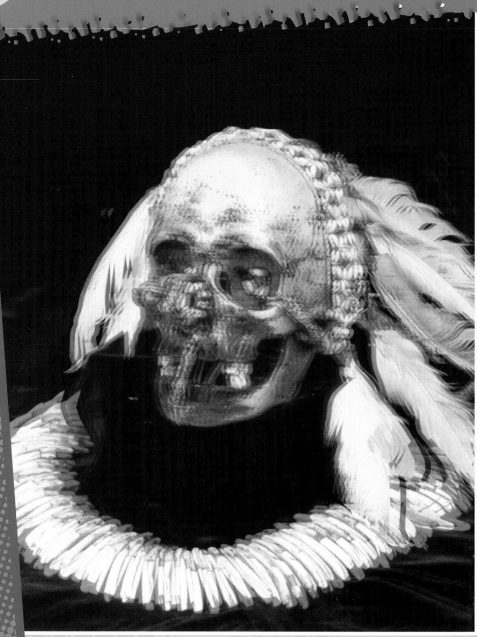

This skull and pig's tooth necklace from New Guinea are among the many grisly artifacts Ripley collected during his world travels.

The process of shrinking a man's head to the size of a baseball had always been a closely guarded secret among the Jivaro Indians of South America—until Robert Ripley obtained the information and revealed it to the world.

The Jivaro sewed the mouths of their shrunken heads shut so the soul, which they believed was trapped inside the head, could not escape.

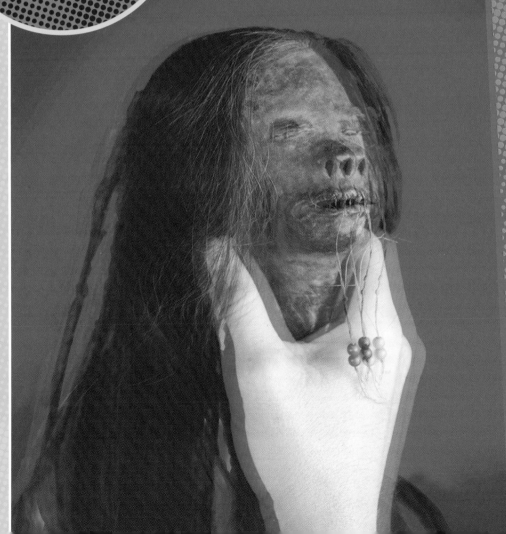

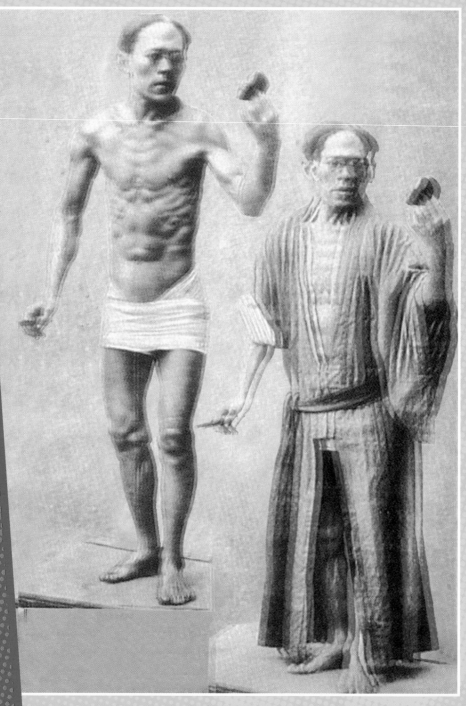

When Hanunama Masakichi, a sculptor of Yokohama, Japan, found out he was dying of tuberculosis, he decided to create an exact replica of himself to leave behind for the woman he loved. His obsession with creating a lifelike statue led him to pluck his own hairs, eyelashes, fingernails, and toenails and affix them to the carved wooden likeness.

When the black plague ravaged Europe in the Middle Ages, a Czech artist named Frantizek Rint found a novel way to make use of the abundance of human bones the plague left behind. He created the Ossuary Chapel of All Saints outside in Sedlac, Czech Republic. The 800-year-old chapel is decorated with elaborate bone chandeliers, chalices, altars, and coats of arms.

Although Ripley insisted on checking the accuracy of all Believe It or Not! claims before they were published, he enjoyed including the occasional well-executed hoax in his personal collection. Ripley owned one of the so-called "Feejee Mermaids." These creepy looking creatures were actually assembled with the head and torso of a monkey stitched to the back half of a dried fish. In the late 19th century, P. T. Barnum, claiming the mermaid was a newly discovered species, put one on display for his audiences who readily believed the fish tale. Even after Barnum's hoax was publicly revealed, Feejee Mermaids continued to appear in souvenir shops in remote parts of the world. Ripley himself picked up his first mermaid in a shop in Macao on the China coast.

Have you got a Believe It or Not! story you'd like to share with the world? If it's wacky or weird enough, the folks at Ripley's would love to hear about it. You can send your Believe It or Not! entries to:

The Director of the Archives
Ripley Entertainment Inc.
5728 Major Boulevard
Orlando, FL 32819